W9-BHO-371

WHY DO WE HAVE DIFFERENT SEASONS?

BY ISAAC ASIMOV

Gareth Stevens Children's Books
MILWAUKEE

For a free color catalog describing Gareth Stevens' list of high-quality children's books, call 1-800-341-3569 (USA) or 1-800-461-9120 (Canada).

Library of Congress Cataloging-in-Publication Data

Asimov, Isaac, 1920-
    Why do we have different seasons? / by Isaac Asimov. — A Gareth Stevens Children's Books ed.
      p. cm. — (Ask Isaac Asimov)
    Includes bibliographical references and index.
    Summary: Describes how the seasons affect people and other living things.
    ISBN 0-8368-0439-2
    1. Seasons—Juvenile literature. [1. Seasons.] I. Title. II. Series: Asimov, Isaac, 1920-
  Ask Isaac Asimov.
  QB637.4.A75 1991
  508—dc20   90-26061

A Gareth Stevens Children's Books edition

Edited, designed, and produced by
Gareth Stevens Children's Books
1555 North RiverCenter Drive, Suite 201
Milwaukee, Wisconsin 53212, USA

Picture Credits
pp. 2-3, Bryan F. Peterson/Third Coast, © 1990; p. 4 (upper), Gini Holland, © 1990; p. 4 (lower), New York State Department of Economic Development; p. 5 (upper), Bryan F. Peterson/Third Coast, © 1989; p. 5 (lower), Bryan F. Peterson/Third Coast, © 1990; pp. 6-7, Mark Mille/DeWalt and Associates; pp. 8-9, Gareth Stevens, Inc.; pp. 10-11, Mark Mille/DeWalt and Associates; p. 12, © Joe Carini/Third Coast; p. 13 (upper), William F. Lemke/Third Coast, © 1985; p. 13 (lower), Gareth Stevens, Inc.; pp. 12-13 (background), New York State Department of Economic Development; pp. 14-15, © Forrest Baldwin; p. 15, Keith Ward; pp. 16-17, Courtesy Michigan Travel Bureau; p. 17, Grant Heilman Photography; p. 18, John Gerlach/DRK Photo; pp. 18-19, S. Nielsen/DRK Photo; pp. 20-21, Japan National Tourist Organization; pp. 22-23, Harry Quinn

Cover photograph, Paul C. Butterbrodt/Third Coast, © 1990: Maple trees turn brilliant colors and shed their leaves during autumn in Milwaukee, Wisconsin.

Series editor: Elizabeth Kaplan
Editor: Patricia Lantier-Sampon
Series designer: Sabine Huschke
Picture researcher: Daniel Helminak
Picture research assistant: Diane Laska
Consulting editor: Matthew Groshek

Printed in MEXICO

1 2 3 4 5 6 7 8 9 97 96 95 94 93 92 91

Contents

Words that appear in the glossary are printed in **boldface** type the first time they occur in the text.

A World of Questions

Our world is full of strange and beautiful things. In some parts of our planet, summer days are long and warm with plenty of sunlight. The flowers are in full bloom.

In autumn, leaves change color and fall from the trees.

Winter days are short and cold. Sometimes snow covers the trees.

In spring, the ground warms up. Flowers blossom and plants begin to grow again.

Other parts of our planet have rainy and dry **seasons**. Whether a place has four seasons or just two, every place has changing seasons. Why do the seasons change? Let's find out.

The Tilting, Turning Earth

Every year, Earth orbits, or circles, once around the Sun. Earth is **tilted** at an angle as it moves in its yearly path. As Earth orbits the Sun, sometimes the northern half of Earth tilts toward the Sun. At other times, the southern half of Earth tilts toward the Sun. The part that is tilted toward the Sun receives more direct light than the part tilted away from the Sun.

Southern part of Earth tilted toward the Sun

Northern part of Earth tilted toward the Sun

Direct and Angled Light

Direct light falls straight on an object. Angled light strikes at a slant. Direct light is stronger than light that shines on an object at an angle. You can see this if you look at the cone of light made by a flashlight.

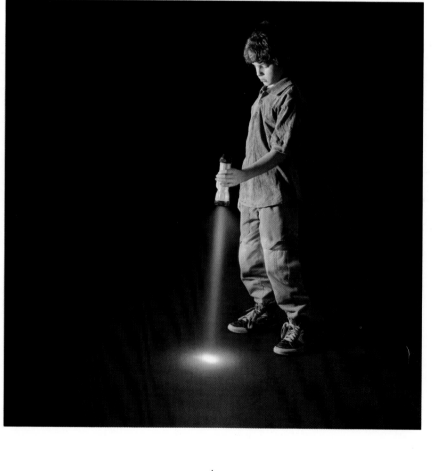

When the flashlight shines directly on an object, it strikes the object with a bright circle of light. When the rays of light strike the object at an angle, the light spreads out more. Then, the object doesn't look as bright. You can see how this works in the pictures on these pages.

angled sunlight

direct sunlight

Sunlight and the Seasons

How sunlight strikes Earth is determined by Earth's tilt. When the northern half of Earth tilts toward the Sun, the Sun's rays hit the Northern Hemisphere straight on, and it is summer.

When the northern half of Earth tilts away from the Sun, the Sun's rays strike the Northern Hemisphere at an angle, as shown. These slanted rays are not as powerful as direct rays, and it is winter.

11

The Topsy-turvy Seasons

Earth doesn't have the same seasons everywhere at the same time. When it is summer in the northern part of the planet, it is winter in the southern part. When it is winter in the northern part, it is summer in the southern part.

Some parts of Earth receive direct sunlight year-round. These parts are near the **Equator**, the imaginary line that divides Earth into a northern and southern half. As you go north and south of the Equator, the seasons become more dramatic.

Summer Days, Winter Nights

In summer, the Sun rises early and sets late.
In winter, it rises later and sets earlier. The
drawings at right show times of sunrise and
sunset on a summer day and a winter day.

In summer at the North Pole, the Sun doesn't
set. During this time of the Midnight Sun,
Earth's tilt keeps the pole in sunlight. The
picture above, taken over a few hours, shows
how the Sun never dips below the horizon.
In winter at the North Pole, the Sun doesn't
rise. Earth's tilt keeps the pole in darkness.

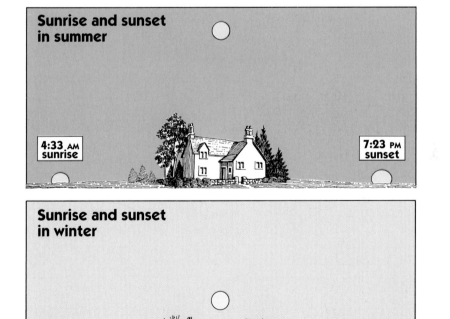

**Sunrise and sunset
in summer**

4:33 AM
sunrise

7:23 PM
sunset

**Sunrise and sunset
in winter**

7:22 AM
sunrise

4:46 PM
sunset

Budding and Blooming

Plants need sunlight and water to grow. That's why summer is the best season for gardening. In winter, there is less sunlight, and water may freeze. Many plants lie **dormant**. They seem dead, but they are still alive. When spring returns, the days become longer and warmer, and the plants bud again.

Some places have dry seasons and wet seasons. In these places, plants are usually dormant in the dry season. They revive with the coming of the rains.

Hibernate, Estivate, or Migrate?

Some animals find it hard to live in cold weather. They lie quietly and **hibernate**, or rest, for the winter. Other animals have trouble surviving hot weather, and they rest during the summer. This is called **estivation**. Squirrels and woodchucks hibernate in the winter. Many animals that live in the desert estivate during hot, dry weather.

Some animals **migrate** before winter arrives. They travel far away from cold weather to warmer places. They usually return in spring. Many birds, including the geese and cranes shown to the right, migrate.

Seasonal Celebrations

Many things depend on changing weather. Farmers plant their crops in spring because that is when seeds grow best. Plants grow during the warm summer months. Crops are **harvested** in autumn, just before the cold winter sets in.

Many holidays and festivals relate to the seasons. In many Western countries, Easter and Passover announce the arrival of spring. In Japan, the Snow Festival celebrates the beauty of snow. Sri Lanka and India have special festivals at the end of the rainy season.

Clues, Clues . . . Everywhere

Keeping track of the seasons is fun! You might notice snow melting on the sidewalk or the sweet scent of lilacs in spring. You might hear the sounds of crisp leaves blowing in the autumn wind. Wherever you live, knowing the signs of changing seasons will help you enjoy the world around you.

22

More Books to Read

I Can Read About Seasons by Robyn Supraner (Troll)
The Seasons by David Lambert (Franklin Watts)
Seasons by Illa Rodendorf (Childrens Press)
Sunshine Makes the Seasons by Franklyn M. Branley (Harper & Row
    Junior Books)
Wonders of the Seasons by Keith Brandt (Troll)
Young Scientists Explore the Seasons by Linda Penn (Good Apple)

Places to Write

Here are some places you can write to for more information
about the seasons and the different types of climates around the
world. Be sure to tell them exactly what you want to know about.
Give them your full name and address so that they can write back
to you.

Association of American
    Weather Observers
P.O. Box 455
Belvidere, Illinois 61008

American Meteorological Society
Education Office
1755 Massachusetts Avenue NW
Suite 700
Washington, D.C.   20036

Canadian Climate Centre
Environment Canada
4905 Dufferin Street
Downsview, Ontario   M3H 5T4

Glossary

dormant (DOOR-ment): to be in a state of sleep or inactivity.

Equator (ee-KWAY-ter): an imaginary line that runs around the
    Earth's center in an east-west direction. The Equator is halfway
    between the North and South poles.

estivation (ESS-tuh-VAY-shun): sleeping or remaining inactive for a long period of time in summer.

harvest (HAHR-vest): to gather a crop that is ripe or ready for use.

hibernate (HIGH-buhr-NAYT): to sleep or remain inactive for a long period of time during winter.

migrate (MY-grayt): to move from one place to another in search of food or warm weather.

season (SEE-zuhn): one of the parts into which a year is divided based on the position of the Earth in relation to the Sun.

tilt: to lean or slant to one side.

Index

24